A Note to Parents

DK READERS is a compelling program for beginning readers, designed in conjunction with leading literacy experts, including Dr. Linda Gambrell, Director of the Eugenge T. Moore School of Education at Clemson University. Dr. Gambrell has served on the Board of Directors of the International Reading Association and as President of the National Reading Conference.

Beautiful illustrations and superb full-color photographs combine with engaging, easy-to-read stories to offer a fresh approach to each subject in the series. Each DK READER is guaranteed to capture a child's interest while developing his or her reading skills, general knowledge, and love of reading.

The four levels of DK READERS are aimed at different reading abilities, enabling you to choose the books that are exactly right for your child:

Level 1 – Beginning to read
Level 2 – Beginning to read alone
Level 3 – Reading alone
Level 4 – Proficient readers

The "normal" age at which a child begins to read can be anywhere from three to eight years old, so these levels are only a general guideline.

LONDON, NEW YORK, DELHI,
MUNICH, AND MELBOURNE

Created by Leapfrog Press Ltd.
Project Editor Naia Bray-Moffatt
Art Editor Jane Horne
For DK Publishing
Senior Editor Mary Atkinson
Managing Art Editor Peter Bailey
U.S. Editor Regina Kahney
Production Melanie Dowland
Picture Researcher Liz Moore
Natural History Consultant
Theresa Greenaway
Reading Consultant
Linda B. Gambrell, Ph.D.

First American Edition, 1999
03 04 05 06 07 10 9 8 7 6 5
Published in the United States by DK Publishing, Inc.
375 Hudson Street, New York, New York 10014

Published in Great Britain by Dorling Kindersley Limited.

Library of Congress Cataloging-in-Publication Data
Chevallier, Chiara
    The secret life of trees / by Chiara Chevallier. -- 1st American ed.
    p.   cm. -- (Dorling Kindersley readers. Level 2)
    Summary: Details the parts and inner lives of trees and all the organisms
that live within them.
    ISBN 0-7894-4761-4 (hc). ISBN 0-7894-4760-6 (pbk.)
    1. Trees--Juvenile literature. 2. Trees--Ecology Juvenile
literature. [1. Trees. 2. Trees--Ecology.--3. Forest ecology.
4. Ecology.] – I. Title. II. Series.
QK475.8.C46 1999
582.16--dc21   99-34117
                                                          CIP
        Color reproduction by Colourscan, Singapore
     Printed and bound in China by L Rex Printing Co., Ltd.

    The publisher would like to thank the following
for their kind permission to reproduce their photographs:
    t=top, a=above, b=below, l=left, r=right, c=center
Bruce Coleman Collection: 6br, 10-11t, 10b, 12cl, cb, lb,
17t, 23br, 27t, b, 32cr, br, 33; Dorling Kindersley Picture Library/
Natural History Museum: 22bl, 28cl, cr, br; Empics: 8br; NHPA: 28;
    Pictor International Ltd: 15br, bl, cr, cl, 26b, 30b, 31;
    Telegraph Colour Library: 4-5, 16, 19t.
Additional photography by: Geoff Brightling, Jane Burton,
Peter Chadwick, Andy Crawford, Steve Gorton, Frank Greenaway,
    Dave King, Karl Shone, James Stevenson, Kim Taylor.
    Modelmakers: Peter Griffiths, Peter Minster/Model FX,
        Chris Reynolds and the BBC Team.
Additional design: Adrienne Hutchinson, Catherine Goldsmith.
        All other images © Dorling Kindersley
    For further imformation see: www.dkimages.com

Discover more at
www.dk.com

DK READERS

The Secret Life of
Trees

Written by Chiara Chevallier

DK Publishing, Inc.

Do you know
the oldest living thing
in the world?

Can you guess
the heaviest living thing
on Earth?

Or the tallest thing alive?

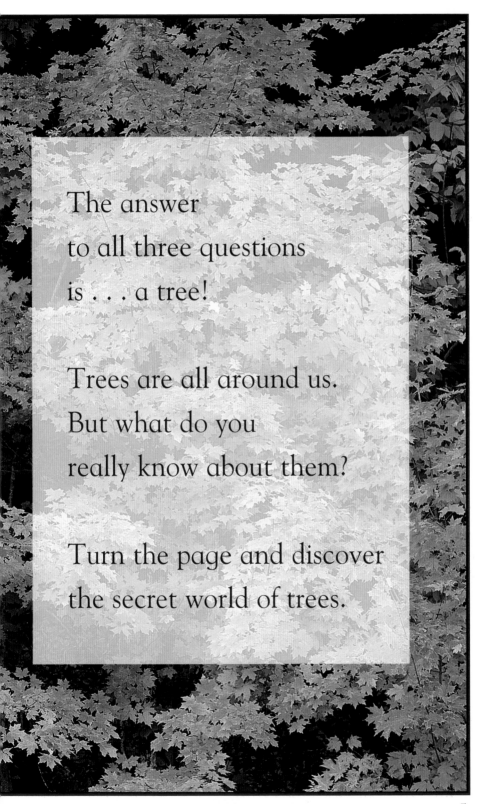

The answer
to all three questions
is . . . a tree!

Trees are all around us.
But what do you
really know about them?

Turn the page and discover
the secret world of trees.

When you look at a tree
what do you see?

You see bark that protects
the tree's trunk and branches.
The bark at the bottom is old.
It is rough and cracked.
At the top the bark
is young and smooth.

The tallest tree
The tallest tree alive today is
over 360 feet high! It is a coast
redwood growing in California.
There is enough wood in its
trunk to build over 300 houses!

When you look at a tree
you can only see half of it!

The other half is underground.
These are the roots,
pushing their way through
the thick earth.

Rooting around

The roots of a tree
that is 150 feet tall,
stretch under the earth
for an area the size of
a soccer field!

They can spread out
through the soil
as far as
the tree is high.

A tree can live longer
than all other living things.
It can live for hundreds –
even thousands – of years!

The oldest tree
The oldest recorded
tree in the world
is a bristlecone pine.
It is an amazing
4,900 years old.

A tree needs
sunlight and water
to grow.

High above the ground,
the tree leaves use energy
from the sun to make food.
Below ground, the tree's roots
spread out in search of water.

When you look at a tree you can see a home for many animals and birds.

High up in the branches, birds carefully build nests. They lay their eggs out of sight and out of reach of other animals.

Under the tree branches, wasps may build a nest.

Insects and bugs live on and under a tree's bark.

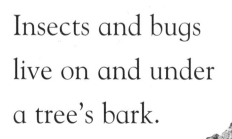

Insect disguise
Some insects, like these
thorn bugs, disguise
themselves as part of a tree
so they don't get eaten.

In the earth,
under the roots of a tree,
rabbits and badgers
dig their homes.

A tree in summer is an animal hotel!

Trees come in all shapes and sizes, but there are two main types:

broad-leaved trees

and conifers.

A broad-leaved tree has large, flat leaves on its wide-spreading branches.

The shady green forests
of eastern North America
are mostly made up
of broad-leaved trees.

Many broad-leaved trees
change their leaves
as the seasons change.

In the cold chill of winter,
most broad-leaved trees
have no leaves.
The leaves have dropped off
because there is less sunlight.

As spring begins,
fresh new leaves open
from buds on the branches.
The tree wakes up
from its winter sleep
as the days get longer
and there is more sunlight.

By summer, the tree is covered
with bright, green leaves.
The leaves give
shade, shelter, and food
to many animals and insects.

As the weather gets colder
in the misty autumn,
the tree's leaves change color.
Some leaves turn brown.
Others turn bright yellow
or brilliant red.
Then they fall
to the ground.
The tree is getting ready
to sleep again until next spring.

New trees are born
when older trees
drop their seeds
on the ground.

A seed faces
many dangers.
Hungry animals
may eat it.

Growing acorns

In one summer,
a fully grown oak tree
can produce up to
50,000 acorns!

It may be stepped on and crushed.

Most seeds never survive

to grow into a tree.

Broad-leaved trees protect their seeds.

Some put them in a hard shell

like an acorn or a chestnut.

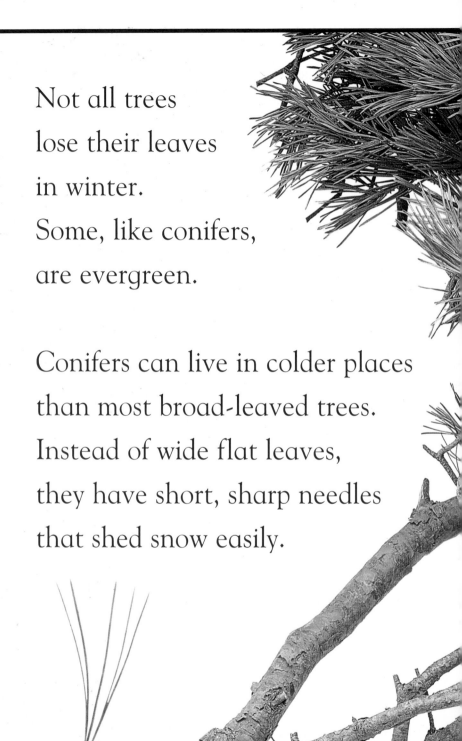

Not all trees
lose their leaves
in winter.
Some, like conifers,
are evergreen.

Conifers can live in colder places
than most broad-leaved trees.
Instead of wide flat leaves,
they have short, sharp needles
that shed snow easily.

Bouncy branches
The branches of a conifer
are extra bouncy. This is so
they don't snap even when
covered with thick snow.

Conifer trees
produce hard,
scaly, cones
to protect their seeds.

Cones come in different sizes.
Some are less than half an inch.
The cone of the sugar pine
is two feet long.

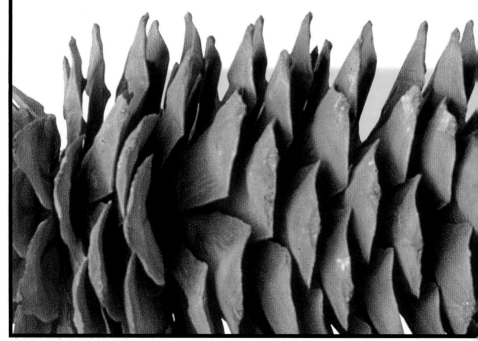

A pine cone can help you forecast the weather! When it is warm, the scales of the cone open up. They close again when a storm is on the way. This is to keep the seeds dry.

Wherever you are in the world
you can usually find
trees growing.

In steamy, wet jungles,
trees grow so close together
that hardly any light
reaches the forest floor.

Thanks to the heat and rainfall, these trees grow faster than other trees – up to 15 feet each year.

Tree houses

In the African forests, chimpanzees spend nearly all their lives up in the trees. They only go down to the jungle floor to look for food.

Tropical trees grow
in the warmest countries
of the world.
Lots of tasty fruits and nuts
come from tropical trees.
Avocados, dates,
mangoes, and Brazil nuts.

Coconut palms grow wild
on the beaches of
many tropical countries.
This palm tree's seed
is inside its hairy
coconut shell.
The shell contains milk
so the seed can start growing
even if it is washed up
somewhere dry.

Killer trees
The seed of the strangler fig
grows in the roots of another
tree. As it grows, its roots
strangle the other tree and cut
out the sunlight until it dies.

When you look at a tree
you can see the source
of wood and paper.

The table you sit at
and the chair
you sit on
may be made of
wood from trees.

The swing
you play on
may be made
from wood.

And the biggest secret of all?
Even the book you are reading
comes from a tree!

Recognizing Trees

The easiest way to recognize a broad-leaved tree is to look at the leaves. The leaves of each type of tree have their own size and shape. Here are the leaves of common trees you might see.

Lime The leaves are heart-shaped with a jagged edge and have long stems. These trees are popular in large gardens.

Ash These feather-like leaves have from three to thirteen leaflets, with the odd one at the end. Ash trees are often planted to line streets.

Horse chestnut The leaves have seven or nine leaflets that point outward like a hand. You might see these trees growing in parks or along streets.

Oak There are many types of oak tree but most have toothed leaves, like this English Oak leaf. These are often found in woods.

Maple Most types of maple leaf are easy to recognize by their handlike shape. In the fall, the leaves often turn a beautiful red.

Holly The holly is evergreen, so even in winter you will find these prickly, shiny green leaves.